A few excerpts from

Chasing Away the Clouds

"Don't lose sight of the one thing that is constant, beautiful, and true: Everything will be fine — and it will turn out that way because of the special kind of person you are."

———————— ■ ————————

"After the rain comes the rainbow. After the hurt comes the healing. Unfolding gently, coming closer every day, this is the natural way of things."

———————— ■ ————————

"Problems and predicaments come to us all. There's no sign saying, 'You must be this tall...' to ride on the emotional roller coasters that take so many of us for a spin. The bad news is that there are times when we're passengers... whether we like it or not. The good news is that we can always choose to get off at the next stop."

———————— ■ ————————

"Nothing wastes more energy than worrying.
The longer one carries a problem, the heavier it gets.
Don't take things too seriously.
Live a life of serenity, not a life of regrets."

Library of Congress Catalog Card Number: 97-36606
ISBN: 0-88396-454-6

■ design on book cover is registered in the U.S. Patent and Trademark Office.

The following works have previously appeared in Blue Mountain Arts publications: "Hang in There," "Twelve Ways to Keep Smiling," "May You Always Have an Angel by Your Side," "Words to Remember," "A Little Morale Booster," and "Twenty-Four Things to Always Remember and One Thing to Never Forget."

Manufactured in the United States of America
First Printing: January, 1998

♻ This book is printed on recycled paper.

Library of Congress Cataloging-in-Publication Data

Pagels, Douglas.
        Chasing away the clouds : words of encouragement that will help you through any hard times and bring more happiness to your life / Douglas Pagels.
            p.   cm.
        ISBN 0-88396-454-6 (alk. paper)
        1. Encouragement   I. Title.
BF637.E53P34   1998
158.1'28--dc21   97-36606
                                                                CIP

Words of encouragement that will
help you through any hard times
and bring more happiness to your life

CHASING

Away the

CLOUDS

by Douglas Pagels

Blue Mountain Press ®

P.O. Box 4549, Boulder, Colorado 80306

This is a book for those who know that life isn't
always easy. It's a travel guide for anyone who wants
to leave hard times behind and move ahead to
brighter days. It's full of practical advice for those
who want to keep a troubled past from turning into
a difficult future. And it's an inspiration for people
who have experienced a loss and who look forward
to the day when they can move beyond its sadness
and into a little more sunshine.

There are many paths that lead to the destinations
of happiness, resolve, and understanding. This book
will walk with you along those paths — sometimes as
an encouraging, loving friend — and other times as a
guiding light. You will find that these writings will have
different meanings during different times in your life,
and that reading a little at a time will help you find
the words in your own heart that serve as companions
to the words in this collection.

The writings and reflections in this book come from
life's circumstances and my own deep beliefs, and they
are dedicated to my friends and loved ones — and to you
and yours — those who do their best to chase away the
clouds and whose journeys are an inspiration to us all.

May your hopes *always* shine through.

— Douglas Pagels

Hang in there

Difficulties arise in the lives of us all.
What is most important is dealing with
the hard times, coping with the changes,
and getting through to the other side
where the sun is still shining just for you.

It takes a strong person to deal with
tough times and difficult choices. But
you are a strong person. It takes courage.
But you possess the inner courage to see
you through. It takes being an active
participant in your life. But you are in
the driver's seat, and you can determine
the direction you want tomorrow to go in.

Hang in there... and take care to see that you don't lose sight of the one thing that is constant, beautiful, and true: Everything will be fine — and it will turn out that way because of the special kind of person you are.

So... beginning today and lasting a lifetime through — hang in there, and don't be afraid to feel like the morning sun is shining... just for you.

———————————— ■ ————————————

As you leave behind all that has been, you are on the way to all that can be.

It hasn't been easy

I know it hasn't been easy. I know there are times when it's tough. I know that things aren't always fair, but that doesn't mean it should be this rough. The journey should be a lot smoother, and life should play by the rules. Time passes too quickly in everything... except when it heals our wounds.

Some days are better than others. Some are a little bit worse. Sometimes everything works out okay. Sometimes it's hard to get past the hurts.

With all my heart, I wish I had more answers. I want to let you know how much I care. I wish the path ahead were clearer to see, and I could walk beside you all the way there.

I want you to have a guardian angel; someone to watch over you. I want you to listen closely to your heart, for it will always speak the truth. I want you to have faith in tomorrow. It will guide your steps today.

And I know that things haven't been easy ...but I <u>know</u> things will be okay.

As one door closes behind you, another will open wide. There's a purpose for this change in your life, and a reason only time will provide.

Twelve ways to keep smiling

Hold on to your dreams, and never let them go. Show the rest of the world what so many people already know: how wonderful you are!

Give circumstances a chance, and give others the benefit of the doubt. Wish on a star that shines in your sky. Take on your problems one by one and work things out.

Rely on all the strength you have inside. Let loose of the sparkle and spirit that you sometimes try to hide. Stay in touch with those who touch your life with love.

Look on the bright side and don't let adversity keep you from winning. Be yourself, because you are filled with special qualities that have brought you this far, and that will always see you through.

Keep your spirits up. Make your heart happy, and let it reflect on everything you do!

———————————— ■ ————————————

When you're chasing away the clouds,
the sky is the limit.

————————————————————————

May you always have an angel by your side

May you always have an angel by your side. Watching out for you in all the things you do. Reminding you to keep believing in brighter days. Finding ways for your wishes and dreams to come true.

Giving you hope that is as certain as the sun. Giving you the strength of serenity as your guide. May you always have love and comfort and courage, and...

May you always have an angel by your side. Someone there to catch you if you fall.

Encouraging your dreams, inspiring your happiness, holding your hand and helping you through it all.

In all of our days, our lives are always changing. Tears come along as well as smiles. Along the roads you travel, may the miles be a thousand times more lovely than lonely. May they give you gifts that never, ever end: someone wonderful to love and a dear friend in whom you can confide. May you have rainbows after every storm. May you have hopes to keep you warm.

And may you always have an angel by your side.

Life is one long process of learning how to earn your wings.
Do your best to be someone who will graduate with flying colors.

Always keep your heart hopeful

Everything will be okay. You'll see.
You're on the way to something better,
and the situation just needs some time
to take you there. Think back to other
moments in your life; to times when you
wondered if you'd ever make it through.
And, in the end, you always did.

Try to think of that now, as you look
within. Give yourself time to experience
everything you're feeling. Time to deal
with emotions and time to...

Take yourself to a place deep down
inside — where you feel the most grounded
and safe and secure. That place is strong
and true, and I have a feeling that it lives in
you more beautifully than you know.

You already understand that help is here
if you need it. But what will help most is
just remembering this:

If you can just give things a chance,
everything will be okay.

I promise.

——————— * ———————

*If your heart's in the right place,
what's left?*

————————————————————

Letting the healing begin

After the rain comes the rainbow. After the hurt comes the healing. Unfolding gently, coming closer every day, this is the natural way of things.

Hard times soften and fade. Hope rises to the surface, and smiles gradually find their way to faces as reminders of some of the precious things tomorrow will surely bring. Life always leads in that direction. Too slowly sometimes, but always towards a more beautiful horizon. After sadness, resolve. After weakness, so much strength. With time and patience as special friends, the tough times pass and the healing begins.

In any difficulty you have known, your heart has always been home to an inner beauty and a special strength. There has been wisdom deep within you, and the more you turn to that wisdom now, the more it will see you through.

When times are tough, I'll wish you strength enough to see your way through anything. When the world brings you uncertainties of which way to go, I'll wish you comforting thoughts and guiding signs and an inner compass that will help you know. I'll wish you a path that is never too long or too hard to travel; a road where help is there if you need it, and a journey that will bring joy to your spirit and peace to your soul.

If you ever need a little reassurance that things are going to be all right, I'll do whatever I can to remind you that... as the rain disappears, the rainbows come again. Serenity unfolds gently, a little more each day, and the healing helps you realize that... everything will be okay.

———————————■———————————

The secret of contentment?
Doing things that are good for the soul.

———————————————————————

Live by your own light, shine by your own star

Promise you'll "remember when..." and have times you'll always "look forward to...." Have a daily conversation with your heart and soul. Take wonderful care... of you.

In the course of time, you will be reminded that hard work gets good results and that keeping healthy is essential. Know when to work your mind and let your body relax, and know when doing just the opposite makes the most sense.

Being able to handle whatever life brings your way is not a matter of coincidence.

Bad decisions come back to haunt you.
Good decisions come back to bless you.

Keep your desires and dreams alive

In time, your guiding lights will take you where you want to go. In time, the days that now seem so difficult will be more gentle. They'll be more forgiving. More understanding. More comforting and calm. You desire serenity, and serenity will come. You dream of leaving hard times behind, and your belief will find itself justified.

As you move ahead, don't be afraid to do what you once thought impossible, even if others don't think you'll succeed. Remember that history is filled with the incredible accomplishments of those who were foolish enough... to believe.

Believing in a brighter day can raise you up more than any difficulties can set you back.

Words to remember

I can barely begin to tell you of all my wishes
for you. There are so many of them, and I
want them all to come true. I want you to
use your heart as a compass as you find your
way in the world. I want to wish you peace of
mind and a peaceful home. I want you to be
self-reliant, self-motivated, and self-sufficient,
but to know that you'll never be alone. I want
you to be safe and smart and cautious. I want
you to be wise beyond your years. I want you
to discover your innermost courage. I want
you to overcome your fears.

Nothing has taken away from this truth: You
are a very special someone. You are a wonderful,
rare person with no comparison. I want you to
know that opportunities will come, and you'll
have many goals to achieve. And the more that
obstacles get in the way of your dreams, the
more you'll need to believe.

Get your feet wet with new experiences, but be sure you never get in over your head. Try to realize how capable you are, and that your possibilities are unlimited. Never give in to negative thinking; it saps your energy for so many other things. And keep responding in a positive way to the challenges life always brings. I pray that you won't rush the future, and that you'll build on the constructive parts of the past.

You have a strong foundation of wonderful qualities... and a joy that will always last.

When you do the things you do with love, you give life a gleam that most people only carry a glimpse of.

Make the most of every day

By being in this moment and living a day at a time, you have access to every gift this world could ever give. This is your moment. Your present, waiting to be unwrapped. Your day in the diary, waiting for a beautiful story, a touch of wonder, a paragraph of progress, a poem of thanks.

When the time comes to close the page on this day, make sure that its story was written just the way the author hoped it would be.

If happiness is the destination, then "This moment in time" *should be the meditation.*

Celebrate all that you are

Amaze yourself with what you discover
you can do. You are capable of miracles of
your own making. The people who share
your space in this world realize that they
are in the presence of someone who is very
special. You need to realize that, too.

You are a wonderful, capable person
whose opportunities will come, whose goals
will be achieved, and who will become a
believer in many beautiful things.

*Volunteer for a worthy cause: Just pause every now and
then... and share a smile with that person in the mirror.*

Discover a more peaceful place within

When life has got you down, remember: it's okay to feel vulnerable. You have a special sense of the truth, and you feel things deeply. Those are truly wonderful qualities to have. What is sometimes perceived as weakness is actually strength. The more you're bothered by something, the more you're empowered to make things right.

One of the things within your power is the ability to set the stage for better days to find you. Put more smiles on your face by discovering more peaceful places within. You know where doubt and pessimism can take you: *Don't go there.* Stay in a place of honor, and uphold that honor with dignity and love. Bring compassion and faith and courage to that space, and even when you're down, things will be looking up.

Where you are can greatly affect what you are.
The right environment can work wonders.

Rest assured that serenity will find you

When you're searching for serenity, do you find it or does it find you? Maybe it's a little of both. You're on the path, your mind is open to the possibilities, your heart is full of hope, and you bump into one another in a way that feels exactly like it was meant to be.

Serenity is knowing that you can do the things that need to be done. You can say the things that need to be said. You can listen to your heart, cross your bridges, and get to the other side of the shore... richer and more rewarded than you ever felt before.

I hope you will be given every reason to believe that...
Whatever life lacks in preventing our sorrows, it
makes up for with thousands of brighter tomorrows.

Remember that tomorrow's sun will shine

Just ahead, beyond any of today's lingering sorrows, is a brand-new vantage point called "tomorrow." When you get there and glance back, make sure you'll be proud of what you see. Make sure you made the most of your opportunities.

Keep the promises you promised yourself. Improve on the things that seemed so difficult in the beginning. Grow in courage and strength and be equal to your tasks. Discover new paths and put disappointment far behind you. And don't ever make the mistake of giving up on your faith: There will come a time when you will be so thankful for having walked through the doors that led to the life you were searching for.

Where should you begin tomorrow morning? At the best and most beautiful point you were able to reach today.

Carry the sun inside you

Within you lives a creative, resourceful person. You have qualities that get better every day. You have the courage and strength to see things through. You have a light that shines inside you. You have known the truth of yesterday, and you have an inner map that will lead the way to a very beautiful tomorrow. You have gifts that have never even been opened and personal journeys waiting to be explored. You have so much going for you.

You are a special person, and you have a future that is in the best of hands. And you need to remember: If you have plans you want to act on and dreams you've always wanted to come true, you have what it takes, because...

You
have
you.

There is an enduring worth to
every positive step you take.

Travel step by step

As with all journeys, the difficult part is simply to begin. Your heart knows what to do; it's up to you to listen to that inner voice. Make your choices carefully and courageously, then take a deep breath and begin. One foot in front of the other, one day at a time, one cloud to push away, one sun to shine.

Travel step by step and reach for one goal before moving ahead to another. That's the way to find out what real accomplishment is. As you go, take it slowly. Your confidence will grow and, in the span of distance and time, you will surprise yourself with the sunlight you'll journey into and the shadows you'll leave behind.

Just don't try to accomplish everything at once. Life is difficult enough without adding frustration to the list.

Journey one day at a time

Today...
How precious it is, and how full of possibilities.
How sad it would be to waste it worrying about
the future, and how wrong it would be to spend
it dwelling on problems from the past.

Today... is here. Today is now.
Today is filled with as much magic as you want
to give it. Today is filled with amazing grace
waiting for you to live it.

*Get rid of any "if only's" and get on with whatever
you need to do to make today your moment in time.*

Never give up hope

Hope is a beautiful answer to many difficult questions. Hope only asks that you believe. Hope only wants you to receive. Hope is "hanging in there" until help arrives. Whenever a day didn't go as planned, hope is there as a comforting guide to help you understand.

Hope is a quiet, personal place where you can always take shelter. Hope is the warm and welcomed knowledge that beautiful possibilities exist. Hope is all these special things, and — in simply knowing this —

When hope is all you've got...
you still have got
a lot.

If you keep planting the seeds of your dreams,
they'll keep trying their best to blossom for you.

Live life in a beautiful way

Live to the fullest, and make each day count.
Don't let the important things go unsaid.
Have simple pleasures in this complex world.
Be a joyous spirit and a sensitive soul.
Take those long walks that would love to be
taken. Explore those sunlit paths that would
love to oblige. Don't just have minutes in the
day; have moments in time. Believe in the new
strength you're discovering inside.

Make tomorrow happier by going there in
ways that really matter. And don't ever
forget that, eventually... dream-chasers
become dream-catchers.

*Work on the "big picture" and turn it
into the masterpiece you know it can be.*

Time is on your side

Realize that what seems so difficult today may be far more manageable tomorrow. And understand — as you're out there trying your hardest and doing your best to make things better — that time is on your side.

You don't just have the next twenty-four hours to make things right. The truth of the matter is...

      you've got

            all the rest

                  of your life.

A life well lived is simply a compilation of days well spent.

Carry on as courageously as you can

Problems and predicaments come to us all. There's no sign saying, "You must be this tall..." to ride on the emotional roller coasters that take so many of us for a spin. The bad news is that there are times when we're passengers... whether we like it or not. The good news is that we can always choose to get off at the next stop.

Know how strong and capable you are. You have weathered times before that had difficulty and frustration. And — just as sure as the sun will rise in the morning — you can rise to this occasion.

The mantra to help you make it through:
"Need to, can do. Have to, will do."

Uncover the undiscovered path

There is a path that will take you exactly
where you want to go. That path is there,
in everyone's life, but it too often goes
undiscovered. It can get overgrown with
distractions and can become hard to find
if our time is spent on too many other things.

Don't be one of the ones who forgets about
its existence. Even though the road will never
appear on any map, you will find your way
there. Your inner strength, your instincts, and
your growing understanding will walk along
beside you. As your gray days disappear in
the distance, each new joy will leave behind
an old sorrow. And, at the close of each new
day, every lesson learned and each question
answered will take you to the beginning of a
brighter tomorrow.

Take more than just the time.
Make more than just a difference.

Tough it out... in a tender way

Don't spend your life climbing the mountain.
Be the mountain. Soft from a distance, but so
much stronger than others imagine you to be.
Toughing it out in a tender way. Enfolding the
seeds of all the dreams you have planted, and
spending each day and all it brings. Knowing
you are capable of riding out any kind of storm.
Taking in the views. Letting the streams flow.

And simply knowing that seasons will pass and
changes will come, but the higher you lift your
spirits... the more you will stand in the sun.

We can always do more than we "think"
we can. Let's think less and imagine more.

Try not to worry

Almost all the wisdom of the world agrees:
worrying doesn't really accomplish anything.
All it does is get in the way of moving on and
making the day brighter.

As tough as life can get, our problems don't get
any lighter by worrying about them. And anxiety
doesn't speed up the process of making everything
right again. The ladders we need to climb are tall
enough as it is; we don't need to make them any
higher. But that's what worrying does; it magnifies
every problem and makes things that are "do-able"
seem so difficult.

Worrying wastes so much energy that should be
spent on other things. It makes you think you're
confronted with a raging river... when you're
actually dealing with a very "wade-able" stream.

---

*If you're narrow-minded about what's to come, you've
already written the story before the dialogue has begun.*

Move ahead

Life continually teaches. We eventually learn. The lessons take their toll on us, but we do survive. It's like getting a degree in hard knocks and finally graduating... to the promise of better days ahead. It's like getting your passport stamped: "Been there, done that, managed to make it through."

There are no guarantees that you won't have to go back to "school" for a refresher course, or that you'll never have to make a difficult journey again. But you're older, wiser, and stronger than before, and it's nice to know you <u>can</u> leave yesterday behind. The price was paid. Now it's time to move ahead — and do the very best you can.

If you can get beyond the problems, you won't make the mistake of paying for them forever
...on the installment plan.

Simple wisdom: Make things nicer than they were. And better than they've been. And when tomorrow comes around — simply do it all over again.

Don't be overwhelmed by stress and sadness

It's hard to have hard times come to those who deserve only smiles. You deserve so much of the sweetness of life and so little of its unhappiness.

Better days are right around the corner, and the best days you will ever know are still ahead. So... don't be overwhelmed by all that is going on. Try to be understanding. Realize that the clouds will pass and so will all of your sorrows. Your smile might be gone for a little while, but I promise: it will reappear in the mirror of a brighter tomorrow.

When sadness comes to you, you need to know that it arrives only as a visitor and not as a permanent guest.

You are worthy of all you seek

You will see your way through this. Whether you're going in search of your bliss or just tending to your most basic needs, you are worthy of all you seek. Your moment to shine is right around the corner. Your period of ascendance will take you places you'll love to be.

The old will change and become the new... in a passage of time that comes to us all. The past we wish to leave behind is left behind, while that which we choose to take with us on our journey is gently folded and placed in our spiritual suitcase and taken along as precious memories.

Happiness is not one big, beautiful jewel we can hold — or lose — in our hands. Each one of us is an hourglass. And in the course of our lives, we get to keep all the diamonds that come our way among the passing sands.

*There are some things no one can give you
...and others that nobody can take away.*

Rise above it

There will always be tough times and difficult days in our lives. It seems like some things weren't meant to be, and some plans just weren't meant to work out. There will always be disappointments to deal with, but there will be so many special blessings, too.

All that is asked of any of us is to try and rise above our problems. Let life show you new ways of doing old things. Let it bring you new discoveries. Let the days introduce you to possibilities you've never known, to dreams you've never dreamed, and to the seeds of ideas you've never sown before.

Let life help you sweeten your beliefs and show you everything hiding just behind the scenes: the deep peace of the changing seasons; the majesty of what it means to have — and be — a friend; the joy to be found in knowing that it's never too late to begin again. Let life bring abundance into your heart and soul. Let it sing in you and show you how to aim for the stars. Let it help you reach out to be all that you are.

It's a pretty simple rule: The more you give... the more you get back. And the more you do that, the more you'll love it.

You're a wonderful person who deserves to have a beautiful life. And if difficulty ever comes along, I know... that you can rise above it.

———————— ■ ————————

What it takes to be a huge success: small, positive steps.

A little morale booster

You're really something, do you know that?
And in spite of whatever may happen in your
day, you are going to stay that way: trying
and giving and living life in the best way you
know how. So keep your spirits up, and keep
things in perspective. It's going to be okay.

You've made it through difficult things before,
right? Right. And you always land on your
feet. Maybe not dancing; maybe not always
sure about what to do next...

But you always manage to figure things out. Especially when you're able to keep your sense of humor and not lose your smile. If you really think about it, you'll realize that you are a very strong individual. Someone who may not have all the answers, but who is at least willing to hope and try and believe.

You can see your way through just about <u>anything</u>; it all depends on how you look at it. And when people look at you, they see someone who really is... pretty amazing.

———————■———————

Whether you're trying to endure
or striving to endeavor,
be the kind of person who can handle
all kinds of "whether."

Believe in this creed

"Twenty-Four Things to Always Remember...
and One Thing to Never Forget"

Your presence is a present to the world.
You're unique and one of a kind.
Your life can be what you want it to be.
Take the days just one at a time.

Count your blessings, not your troubles.
You'll make it through whatever comes along.
Within you are so many answers.
Understand, have courage, be strong.

Don't put limits on yourself.
So many dreams are waiting to be realized.
Decisions are too important to leave to chance.
Reach for your peak, your goal, your prize.

Nothing wastes more energy than worrying.
The longer one carries a problem,
   the heavier it gets.
Don't take things too seriously.
Live a life of serenity, not a life of regrets.

Remember that a little love goes a long way.
Remember that a lot... goes forever.
Remember that friendship is a wise investment.
Life's treasures are people... together.

Realize that it's never too late.
Do ordinary things in an extraordinary way.
Have health and hope and happiness.
Take the time to wish upon a star.

And don't ever forget...
   for even a day... how very special you are.

———■———
It all adds up.

This is how it works

Each new day is a blank page in the diary
of your life. The pen is in your hand, but
the lines will not all be written the way you
choose; some will come from the world and
the circumstances that surround you. But
for the many things that <u>are</u> in your control,
there is something special you need to know.

The secret of life is in making your story as
beautiful as it can be. Write the diary of
your days and fill the pages with words that
come from the heart.

As the pages take you through time, you
will discover paths that will add to your
happiness and your sorrows, but if you can
do these things, there will always be hope
in your tomorrows...

Follow your dreams. Work hard. Be kind.
This is all anyone could ever ask: Do what
you can to make the door open on a day
that is filled with beauty in some special way.

Remember: Goodness will be rewarded.
Smiles will pay you back. Have fun. Find
strength. Be truthful. Have faith. Don't
focus on the things you lack.

Realize that people are the treasures in
life, and happiness is the real wealth.
Have a diary that describes how you did
your best, and...

The rest will take care of itself.

—————————— ■ ——————————

*Don't be afraid to feel like the morning
sun is shining... just for you.*

————————————————

About the author

Douglas Pagels has been one of Blue Mountain Arts'
favorite writers for many years. His philosophical
sayings and sentiments on friendship and love have
been translated into seven languages and shared with
millions of people worldwide in notecards, calendars,
and his previous books. He lives in the mountains of
Colorado with his wife and two sons.